'THE CLOUD-CAPPED TOWERS'

Published by Sir John Soane's Museum
13 Lincoln's Inn Fields, London WC2A 3BP
www.soane.org

Registered Charity No. 313609
Text and images © Sir John Soane's Museum, 2016, unless otherwise indicated
ISBN 978-0-9932041-2-8

Catalogue design by VERMILL0N
Printed by Gráficas Castuera

Front cover: Soane office Royal Academy Lecture drawing, elevation of the
Shakespeare Gallery (detail), *c.*1806–15, SM 18/7/14

Back cover: Adam office, elevation of a proscenium for the Drury Lane Theatre
(detail), 1775, SM Adam volume 27/85

SIR JOHN
SOANE'S
MUSEUM
LONDON

'THE CLOUD-CAPPED TOWERS':
Shakespeare in Soane's Architectural Imagination

Contents

All quotations from Shakespeare are taken from
The Oxford Shakespeare second edition, 2005.

Left: Bust of William Shakespeare,
plaster, n.d., SM L62

Architectural responses to Shakespeare in the Georgian period

Frances Sands

Georgian Britain saw a renaissance of Shakespeare's plays thanks, in part, to the actor David Garrick. To any educated Georgian such as Sir John Soane, knowledge of Shakespeare was to be expected. Indeed, Soane quoted Shakespeare with some regularity in his lectures at the Royal Academy:

> *The cloud-capped towers, the gorgeous palaces,*
> *The solemn temples, the great globe itself –*
> *Yea, all which it inherit, shall dissolve*[1]

This excerpt from *The Tempest* was used by Soane to illustrate the permanence of ancient Egyptian architecture. In his own words:

> *Such indeed is the solidity of the public works in general of the Egyptians that neither time nor the convulsions of nature, nor the revolutions of empires have destroyed them, nor the power of merciless and extirpating conquerors removed.*[2]

Other essays in this book consider Soane's engagement with Shakespearean performance, bardolatry and the theme of Shakespeare which permeates Soane's collection, but what of Shakespeare's influences over Soane's architectural output and drawings collection? While Soane's characteristic aesthetic was profoundly theatrical, a direct correlation between the work of Shakespeare and Soane's architecture is difficult to establish, especially as Soane was not an architect of theatres. However, if we consider Soane as a man of his time (1753–1837) and one influenced by the Georgian resurgence of Shakespeare, then we can observe the architecture made possible by the Shakespeare movement. This essay seeks to examine some of the key architectural responses to Shakespeare in the Georgian period. It will consider the architectural patronage of Garrick – the drawings for which survive within Soane's collection – as well as the popularity of Georgian Shakespeare-themed history paintings, many of which depict actors such as Garrick, and resulted in the construction of the Shakespeare Gallery by George Dance, a building which heavily inspired Soane when he designed Dulwich Picture Gallery.

David Garrick: an introduction

David Garrick (1717–79), the son of an impoverished army officer, left the family home in Lichfield in 1737 in the company of his friend and onetime tutor Samuel Johnson and walked to London with the intention

Left: Fig. 1. William Hogarth, *David Garrick as Richard III*, (detail), 1745, WAG 634. Courtesy National Museums Liverpool

of studying law.[3] His legal studies at Lincoln's Inn lasted just a few days and instead he joined his brother Peter as a vintner with cellars in Durham Yard off the Strand.[4] Despite being a largely unsuccessful venture, it was through this profession that Garrick became acquainted with various theatre managers and in 1740 began working as an amateur playwright and actor, acting professionally from 1741. His first plaudits came playing Richard III at Goodman's Fields Theatre on 19 October 1741 (Fig. 1).[5] Garrick's work as a playwright was compatible with Georgian taste but it was his acting abilities which propelled him to notoriety. He was credited with an ability to imbue characters with unprecedented naturalism and sincere emotions, becoming particularly popular as a tragedian specialising in Shakespearean characters.

Interest in Shakespeare had blossomed in London since the 1730s, when the Shakespeare Ladies Club successfully lobbied for Shakespearean performances.[6] Garrick credited the Shakespeare Ladies Club with the restoration of Shakespeare to the London stage, writing in Shakespeare's name: 'the Ladies of Great Britain were so earnest to prop the sinking State of Wit and Sense, that they form'd themselves into a Society, and reviv'd the Memory of the forsaken Shakespear.'[7] However, it was Garrick himself who played a larger role in popularising Shakespeare, even deifying the playwright – 'the god of our idolatry' as Garrick called him – when he organised the first Shakespeare festival, the Shakespeare Jubilee at Stratford-upon Avon in September 1769.[8] Although not the first to study Shakespeare, it was Garrick's friend, Dr Samuel Johnson, who is credited with stimulating the widespread criticism of Shakespeare.[9] Between them, Garrick and Johnson set about attempting to purify and authenticate Shakespeare's work, but also, conversely, to render it less esoteric by amending terminology and plotlines to suit Georgian audiences.[10]

In 1747 Garrick invested £12,000 in a half-share of the patent of the Drury Lane Theatre in partnership with James Lacy; whereby Lacy would manage the property and Garrick the stage. This arrangement endured until Lacy's death in 1774 and provided Garrick with an annual payment of £500 in proprietor's expenses and a 500 guinea salary for acting.[11] He contracted over 300 actors and developed the Theatre into the most popular in London.[12] On his retirement in 1776, Garrick sold his half-share of the theatre's lease for £35,000 to Dr James Ford, Thomas Linley and Richard Brinsley Sheridan.[13] Garrick died only three years later from kidney failure.[14] His magnificent funeral included a cortege of 36 carriages travelling from Garrick's house on the Adelphi to Westminster Abbey, where he was buried in Poet's Corner.[15]

Garrick as architectural patron

Sir John Soane's interest in Garrick extended beyond his enthusiasm for theatre or the wider public's admiration and into architectural design. Within Soane's drawings collection there are designs for schemes commissioned by Garrick from the neo-classical architect Robert Adam. In 1833, Soane acquired the Adam office drawings collection from the Adam brothers' niece, Susanna Clerk, for £200.[16] Among these were designs for three houses owned by Garrick and – perhaps most importantly – for the Drury Lane Theatre itself.

The plot between Drury Lane and Catherine Street on which the Theatre is found, has been the location of a theatre longer than any other in London.[17] The original theatre – known as the Theatre Royal on Brydges Street – was built in 1662–63 to designs by an unknown architect for Thomas Killgrew and the King's Company.[18] The original fabric was destroyed by fire in 1672 and rebuilt over the next two years to designs by Christopher Wren (1632–1723).[19] It re-opened as the Theatre Royal on Drury Lane and therein lies the origin of the name which survives to this day.[20]

In 1775, just a year before his retirement, Garrick commissioned Adam to Georgianise the Theatre, giving it a new façade and interior. Adam's design for the proscenium and two alternative schemes for the ceiling of the auditorium survive within Soane's collection (Figs 2-4).[21] The proscenium design is ornamented with a cameo of Shakespeare and shows a structure of 28 by 21 feet 5 inches, giving an idea of the auditorium's size, but it is not known if it was executed. The executed 1775 scheme for the ceiling, showing a coffered dome and oval oculus, was achieved in *trompe l'oeil* and necessitated raising the ceiling height by 20 feet.[22] Adam's later, 1776 compartmental ceiling design suggests an intention to repaint but this was never done. Although Adam's

Opposite page top: Fig. 2. Adam office, elevation of a proscenium for the Drury Lane Theatre, 1775, SM Adam volume 27/85

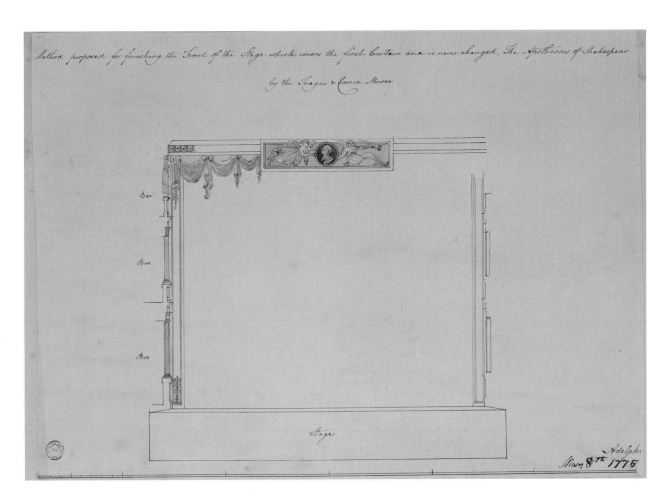

Fig. 3. Adam office, executed plan of a ceiling for the Drury Lane Theatre, 1775, SM Adam volume 14/17

Fig. 4. Adam office, unexecuted plan of a ceiling for the Drury Lane Theatre, (detail), 1776, SM Adam volume 14/16

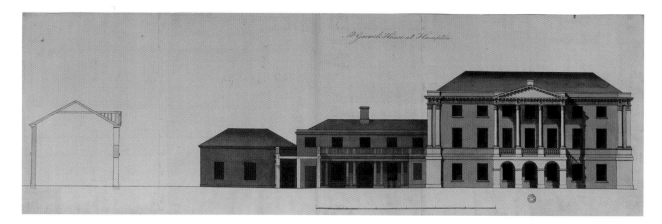

Fig. 5. Adam office, elevation showing alterations to
Hampton House, *c.*1774–75, SM Adam volume 42/58

work at the Drury Lane Theatre was dictated by the
pre-existing fabric, he was certainly proud of the
scheme, including both the design for the façade and
the executed interior in his publication, *The Works in
Architecture of Robert and James Adam*.[23] Adam's work
does not survive as the theatre has since been rebuilt
on two occasions.[24]

Away from the theatre, and as a private patron,
Garrick was generous to Adam. In 1749 Garrick
married a Viennese dancer, Eva Maria Veigel
(1724–1822)[25] and five years later in 1754 they first
rented and then purchased Fuller House at Hampton-
on-Thames, later known as Hampton House. The
origins of the house are unknown but it appears to
date from the seventeenth century.[26] With its six acres
of Brownian landscape, Hampton became Garrick's
haven away from the theatre.[27] In 1755 he also built his
Temple to Shakespeare there: an octagonal and domed
structure with Ionic columns housing a sculpture of
Shakespeare by Louis-François Roubiliac, and made
famous by Johann Zoffany's 1762 painting, *The Temple
to Shakespeare at Hampton House with Mr and Mrs
Garrick* (see p.20). Various scholars have suggested that
the Temple was designed in 1755 by a young Robert
Adam, but this is unlikely as Adam left Britain in late
1754 to embark on a Grand Tour and did not return
until 1758. In 1774–75 Adam was commissioned to
make improvements to Hampton. He extended the
fabric, refaced it with stucco, added Spalatro capitals
to the portico, and decorated some of the interiors (Fig.
5).[28] The house survives, and is now divided into flats.

In 1757 Garrick acquired another country
property, Hendon Hall in Barnet for £13,038.[29]
This was an investment and Garrick undertook no

alterations to the mid-eighteenth-century Palladian
villa[30] – which is now much altered – but did
commission Adam to design a two-arch picturesque-
style bridge for the park, although this was not
executed.[31] Adam's drawing is undated, but the bridge
commission was presumably contemporary with the
mid-1770s work at Hampton.

Garrick's London home had been 27 Southampton
Street since 1743. Then, on 1 June 1771, he acquired
a 96-year lease of 5 Royal Terrace (Fig. 6).[32] This was
part of the Adelphi, a large-scale speculative scheme
of houses, warehouses and shops by the Adam
brothers[33], and comprised a four-storey, three-bay
terraced house, set over a double basement and with
a view over the Thames. Coincidentally, the Adelphi
was built on Durham Yard, the site of Garrick's wine
cellars in the 1730s. Garrick was the first resident
of the Adelphi, moving into his house by April
1772[34] but immediately on signing the lease in 1771,
Garrick allowed Adam to use his name to advertise
the Adelphi in *Town and Country Magazine*: 'one of
the centre houses is purchased by Mr Garrick, and is
almost completely fitted up in a truly classic style'.[35]
Three years later Adam became Garrick's neighbour
when he moved into 4 Royal Terrace.

A Georgian townhouse would typically be arranged
with a dining room in the front ground-floor room,
with a parlour or library-cum-dressing room behind,
and drawing rooms above. Plans of Garrick's house –
made by the Adam office for promotional purposes
– show that the rooms on the ground floor of 5 Royal
Terrace had been reversed, with a dressing room
(Garrick's library) at the front overlooking the Thames,
and the dining room behind.[36] This was most unusual,

Fig. 6. Adam office, elevation of 5 Royal Terrace, Adelphi, *c.*1768–70, SM Adam volume 42/60

as it afforded a better view to the more private of the two rooms. It is recorded anecdotally that this was Garrick's own doing in order to provide himself with a fine outlook while he was writing. Unfortunately, the house was demolished in 1936.

Further to these works, following Garrick's death in 1779, Adam also produced three unexecuted designs for a monument to Garrick, commissioned by their mutual acquaintance Sir Watkin Williams Wynn for the park at Wynnstay Hall, Denbighshire.[37]

The influence of the Shakespeare Gallery
Admiration of Garrick continues to this day. The Garrick Club was founded in 1831; intended as a place for social and literary discourse among 'actors and men of refinement and education'. Soane became

a member in its first year.[38] The Club possesses a large collection of theatrical paintings, including several depicting Garrick himself. On account of his celebrity, Garrick was represented in more paintings than any other person in Georgian Britain save King George III.[39] Many of these works depicted Garrick *en rôle*. Some of the most significant surviving Garrick portraits include William Hogarth's *David Garrick as Richard III* (1745) (Fig. 1); Sir Joshua Reynolds' *David Garrick between Tragedy and Comedy* (1761) and *David Garrick as Kitely* (1767); Pompeo Batoni's *David Garrick* (1764); Angelica Kauffman's *David Garrick* (1764); and Thomas Gainsborough's *David Garrick* (1770–71).

Excepting stage scenery, there was little tradition of theatrical painting in the early eighteenth century.[40] It was Hogarth's *David Garrick as Richard III* which simultaneously affirmed Garrick's public image, and sparked an interested in Shakespearean history painting[41]: Charles Grignon's 1746 engraving of the painting became the most popular theatrical portrait of the Georgian period.[42] History painting is a genre defined by subject matter depicting a tableau from within a narrative, for example a scene from mythology or the Bible. The traditional hierarchy of art places history painting as the most refined, a concept advocated by Sir Joshua Reynolds on 10 December 1771 in his fourth Discourse delivered to the Royal Academy in which he referred to the 'great style': 'I call this part of the art History Painting; it ought to be called Poetical, as in reality it is.'[43] Moreover, in the artist's choice of subject for history painting Reynolds informed the Academy, 'Invention in Painting does not imply the invention of the subject; for that is commonly supplied by the Poet or Historian.'[44] The foundation of the Royal Academy in 1768 coincided with Garrick's Shakespeare Jubilee a year later, and offered artists a forum in which to exhibit their work to potential clients who were inevitably also attending the theatre.[45] From the 1740s onwards, history painting came to include theatrical subject matters, allowing artists who were otherwise shackled by the bread and butter of portraiture, to tap into the popularity of celebrity actors such as Garrick.[46] This was buoyed by the newfound prominence of Shakespeare on the stage, the publication of illustrated Shakespeare editions, and an escalating commercialisation of art through the sale of engravings.[47] Evidence for the appreciation

Fig. 7. Soane office Royal Academy lecture drawing, elevation of the Shakespeare Gallery, *c.*1806–15, SM 18/7/14

of theatrical engravings can be seen in a letter from David Garrick to his brother George, written in Paris on 20 November 1764: 'I am so plagu'd here for my Prints or rather Prints of Me – that I must desire You to send by ye first opportunity six prints from Reynolds' picture...'[48]

The leading print seller of the age was Alderman John Boydell (1720–1804). The eldest of seven children of a land steward, Josiah Boydell, John Boydell began his career as an engraver apprenticed to William Harry Toms in 1740.[49] Moderate success enabled him to establish a print selling business from a shop on Cheapside in 1751, and having taught himself French he was able to build a large international market.[50] Lucrative publications of collected prints allowed Boydell to move his shop to larger premises on the corner of Cheapside and Ironmonger Lane, where he assembled an emporium of prints, and also – unusually for a print seller – he exhibited paintings.[51] This was a lavish exercise, and frames were commissioned from Robert Adam.[52] Boydell became an alderman in 1782, serving in several offices and was even selected as Lord Mayor in 1790–91.[53] In November 1786, Boydell's nephew and business partner, Josiah held a dinner at his home in Hampstead with guests including George Romney, Paul Sandby, Benjamin West and John Boydell himself, and together this group devised the concept of an art gallery dedicated to Shakespeare.[54] Tapping into the demand for Shakespearean history painting, the idea was to establish a permanent exhibition and achieve financial self-sufficiency for the collection through the sale of prints.[55] Inevitably, others aped this formula including Thomas Macklin's Poet's Gallery of 1788, Robert Bowyer's Historic Gallery of 1792, James Woodmason's Irish Shakespeare Gallery of 1794, and Henry Fuseli's Milton Gallery of 1799.[56]

The Shakespeare Gallery was built in 1788–89 at 52 Pall Mall to designs by George Dance the Younger, and was only the second purpose-built art gallery in England.[57] The 25-foot wide façade comprises two double-height storeys with a pediment. It is ornamented with Dance's specifically designed ammonite order pilasters and a tablet by Thomas Banks showing *The Apotheosis of Shakespeare* (Fig. 7). The building contained a generous entrance hall, giving access to a stone staircase to the principal galleries on the first floor.[58] These were an enfilade of three rooms connected by arches, and top-lit with

Fig. 8. Soane office Royal Academy lecture drawing, detail of the ammonite capital from the Shakespeare Gallery, *c.*1806–15, SM 24/2/10

rectangular lanterns, giving even light and greater wall space for hanging.[59] The ground-floor rooms were used as a commercial gallery for the display of drawings and prints after the exhibits above.[60]

None of Dance's drawings for the building survive, but it had caught the attention of Soane – Dance's one-time pupil – who used it to illustrate his Royal Academy lectures. An elevation of the façade to Pall Mall was used by Soane in his fourth lecture to criticise the 'strange and extravagant absurdity' of utilising a massive entablature supported by non-structural pilasters.[61] Despite this, the ammonite capital which had been devised by Dance specifically for these pilasters is the subject of another drawing (Fig. 8)[62] and was praised by Soane in his third lecture:

The beautiful capital in the drawing before you is so well conceived in all its parts, and so truly in the grand style of antiquity that it is impossible for any man with the least spark of knowledge of architecture, or with any love of the art, not to feel highly gratified with this production of successful genius.[63]

Watkin has suggested that the ammonite capital may have been inspired by a plate from Piranesi's *Diverse maniere…* (1769).[64] However, there is no known iconographical purpose, metaphorical reasoning or Shakespearean relevance to Dance's use of the ammonite motif.

On opening to the public in May 1789, there were 34 paintings in the Gallery by artists including Henry Fuseli, Angelica Kauffman, James Northcote and Joshua Reynolds.[65] Over its sixteen-year history, the Gallery amassed 167 paintings. Boydell's plan to support the Gallery through the sale of prints was unsuccessful owing both to Josiah's choice of low-quality stipple engravings and the collapse of the

Above: Fig. 9. James Durno, *Merry Wives of Windsor: Falstaff in disguise led out by Mrs Page,* 1788, SM P211

Opposite page: Fig. 10. Soane office, view showing the interior of Dulwich Picture Gallery, (detail), 1811, SM 65/4/14

international print market with the French Revolution; by 1803 Boydell had accrued a debt of £41,000.[66] In order to offset this debt, in 1804 – the year of Boydell's death – a private act of Parliament enabled a lottery of the Gallery contents. Halted by Boydell's death, the lottery never took place and a year later many of the paintings were placed in a sale at Christie's. Both the 'Plan of the Shakespeare Lottery' from 1804 and the Christie's sale catalogue of 1805 survive in Soane's collection.[67] Moreover, Soane acquired two paintings from the Shakespeare Gallery at Christie's: William Hamilton's *Richard II* and James Durno's *Merry Wives of Windsor* (Fig. 9).[68]

The Shakespeare Gallery was a commercial failure but it established a new British school of art and Boydell's engravings – albeit often altered – continued

to appear in illustrated editions of Shakespeare throughout the nineteenth century.[69] Dance's gallery building was leased in 1805 to the newly founded British Institution as an exhibition space, but in c.1868 the building was demolished in favour of the Marlborough Club which now serves as offices.[70] Despite its forfeiture, the building itself was almost as influential as the art it had been built to contain, and not least to Soane.

In 1811 Sir Francis Bourgeois bequeathed his collection of paintings, as well as those he had inherited from Noel Desenfans to Dulwich College, providing funds for the construction of a new gallery to designs by Soane.[71] Soane's 1811 design for the Dulwich Picture Gallery was certainly derived from traditional long galleries in country houses, but was also clearly inspired by Dance's Shakespeare Gallery.[72] The Shakespeare Gallery contained an enfilade of three rooms connected by arches and top-lit with rectangular lanterns, while Soane's Dulwich Picture Gallery originally contained an enfilade of five rooms connected by arches and top-lit with octagonal lanterns (Fig. 10). Dulwich Picture Gallery has been altered since Soane's work, but remains one of the abiding influences over gallery architecture. Doubtless Soane's design would not have taken this exact form – this quintessential gallery form – had he not been inspired by Dance's work at the Shakespeare Gallery.

The path from Shakespeare to Soane, via Garrick and Boydell is perhaps a tenuous one. However, the influence of the Shakespeare Gallery over Soane's work at Dulwich must not be overlooked. Nor can the two paintings from the Shakespeare Gallery which were acquired by Soane for his own collection. Soane's architectural drawings collection is peppered with projects made possible by the Georgian Shakespeare revival: Garrick's architectural patronage of Adam providing the most notable examples. An ability to quote Shakespeare was characteristic of any educated gentleman contemporary with Soane, but these architectural responses from among Soane's collection are surely proof of a deeper engagement with Shakespeare than is otherwise immediately obvious from Soane's architectural output.

Dr Frances Sands is Curator of Drawings and Books at Sir John Soane's Museum.

Endnotes

1   S. Wells and G. Taylor (eds), *The Oxford Shakespeare: The Complete Works*, 2005, p. 1238: *The Tempest*, Act 4, Scene 1, lines 152-54.

2   D. Watkin, *Sir John Soane: Enlightenment thought and the Royal Academy Lectures*, 1996, p. 497.

3   I. McIntyre, *Garrick*, 1999, p. 27.

4   P. Thomson, 'Garrick, David (1717-1779)', *Oxford Dictionary of National Biography*, Oxford, 2004: http://www.oxforddnb.com/view/article/10408?docPos=1 (accessed 07-01-16). [hereafter Thomson, DNB]

5   J. Benedetti, *David Garrick and the Birth of Modern Theatre*, 2001, p. 47.

6   E.L. Avery, 'The Shakespeare Ladies Club', *Shakespeare Quarterly*, Volume 7, Spring 1956, pp. 153-58.

7   *Daily Advertiser*, 26 May 1737; quoted in Avery, 1956, p. 155.

8   M. Walsh, *Shakespeare, Milton & Eighteenth-Century Literary Editing*, 1997, p. 117.

9   Samuel Johnson's *The Plays of William Shakespeare* (1765) was the first comprehensive assemblage of Shakespeare's work, and set a new standard by which literary criticism of Shakespeare should be undertaken. C. Luppo McDaid, *Shakespeare in the 18th century: Johnson, Garrick and friends* exhibition at Dr Johnson's House (August-November 2015).

10   Luppo McDaid, 2015.

11   McIntyre, 1999, pp. 132-133.

12   Thomson, DNB.

13   *Survey of London*, Volume XXXV, 1970, p. 16.

14   McIntyre, 1999, p. 607.

15   Benedetti, 2001, p. 225.

16   A.A. Tait, 'The Sale of Robert Adam's Drawings', *The Burlington Magazine*, Volume 120, July 1978, pp. 451-54.

17   R. Carter, 'The Drury Lane Theatres of Henry Holland and Benjamin Dean Wyatt', *Journal of the Society of Architectural Historians*, Volume 26, October 1967, p. 200.

18   *Survey of London*, 1970, p. 9.

19   Ibid.

20   Carter, 1967, p. 200.

21   SM Adam volumes 27/85 & 14/16-17.

22   A. Kendall, *David Garrick: A Biography*, 1985, p. 169.

23   R. and J. Adam, *The works in architecture of Robert and James Adam*, Volume II, 1779, part V, plates vi-vii.

24 There are various drawings within the Soane collection for later work on the Drury Lane Theatre: SM 61/3/1-36.

25 H.R. Smith, *The Story of Garrick and his life at Hampton*, 1998, p. 2.

26 D. King, *The Complete Works of Robert and James Adam*, 2001, p. 207.

27 McIntyre, 1999, p. 216.

28 SM Adam volumes 42/58-59.

29 Thomson, DNB.

30 B. Cherry, and N. Pevsner, *The Buildings of England: London 4: North*, 1998, p. 165.

31 SM Adam volume 51/26.

32 *Alan G. Thomas* sale catalogue number 18, 1967, p. 17.

33 SM Adam volume 32/10.

34 Fanny Burney recorded in her diary that she visited Garrick at the Adelphi in April 1772. D.G.C. Allan, *The Adelphi: Past and Present*, 2001, p. 42.

35 Allan, 2001, p. 38.

36 SM Adam volumes 42/60-67.

37 SM Adam volumes 1/250 and 44/83-84.

38 Sir John Soane's Museum, *A Complete Description*, 2014, p. 111.

39 D. Shawe-Taylor, '"The Beautiful Strokes of a Great Actor": Garrick and his painters', in *Every Look Speaks: Portraits of David Garrick*, 2003, p. 11.

40 F. Ritchie, and P. Sabor (eds), *Shakespeare in the Eighteenth Century*, 2012, p. 227.

41 Lesser known, but probably the earliest theatrical paintings are Hogarth's *Falstaff examining his Troops* (1728) and his *Scenes from 'The Tempest'* (1730s). J. Martineau et al., *Shakespeare in Art*, 2003, p. 50.

42 Ibid. p. 12.

43 J. Reynolds, 'Discourse IV', 10 December 1771 in *The Works of Sir Joshua Reynolds*, 1798, pp. 85-86.

44 Ibid. p. 80.

45 Ritchie, 2012, p. 229.

46 Ibid. p. 236.

47 Ibid. p. 229.

48 Quoted in Martineau, 2003, p. 115.

49 T. Clayton, 'Boydell, John (1720-1804)', *Oxford Dictionary of National Biography*, Oxford, 2004: http://www.oxforddnb.com/view/article/3120?docPos=1 (accessed 07-01-16). [hereafter Clayton, DNB]

50 Ibid.

51 R. Dias, *Exhibiting Englishness: John Boydell's Shakespeare Gallery and the Formation of a National Aesthetic*, 2013, p. 17.

52 SM Adam volumes 20/253-55.

53 Clayton, DNB.

54 Martineau, 2003, p. 97.

55 Boydell's 1803 print catalogue survives in the Soane Museum archive. SM 5054.

56 Dias, 2013, p. 24.

57 J. Lever, *Catalogue of the Drawings of George Dance the Younger and of George Dance the Elder*, 2003, pp. 154-55.

58 Dias, 2013, p. 49.

59 Top lighting of galleries was relatively innovative in Britain, and only began to appear in the galleries of private houses from *c.*1795. Dance would later use circular lanterns in the museum of the Royal College of Surgeons, Lincoln's Inn Fields in 1805-12. Lever, 2003, p. 156.

60 Dias, 2013, p. 49.

61 Watkin, 1996, p. 536. SM 18/7/14.

62 SM 24/2/10.

63 Watkin, 1996, p. 517.

64 Ibid.

65 Martineau, 2003, p. 99.

66 Clayton, DNB.

67 SM Private Correspondence V.I.11.1 and SM 1535.

68 Soane, 2014, p. 108.

69 P. Cannon-Brookes, *The Painted Word: British History Painting: 1750-1830*, 1991, p. 40.

70 Lever, 2003, p. 156.

71 D. Stroud, *Sir John Soane Architect*, 1984, p. 200.

72 SM 65/4/14 & 17.

John Soane, Bardolater[1]

Alison Shell

The eighteenth and early nineteenth centuries saw the growth and consolidation of the notion that Shakespeare stood head and shoulders above other English writers.[2] This heightening of Shakespeare's reputation encouraged the habit of using quasi-religious language for the man and his works; during the Shakespeare Jubilee of 1769 at Stratford-upon-Avon, the actor David Garrick declared, in an ode nicely poised between irony and seriousness: "'Tis he! 'Tis he! - that demi-god! / Who Avon's flow'ry margin trod, / ... 'Tis he! 'Tis he! / "The god of our idolatry!"".[3]

By the time that John Soane was devising his museum and putting together his collections, the phenomenon we now call bardolatry was well established, and had been reinforced by other cultural shifts.[4] In the ideological and cultural aftermath of the French Revolution, the veneration of great men in place of God had become a familiar idea: Jacques-Germain Soufflot's Panthéon, a building serially repurposed as a church and a secular mausoleum, stands as emblematic of it.[5] Soane's museum featured tributes to many of his heroes, among them Napoleon and William Pitt the younger, and one can see it as, among much else, a personal Panthéon.[6]

Soane's admiration for Shakespeare is evident in the Museum's many paintings depicting Shakespearean subjects, and in his acquisition of the First Folio and other Shakespeare-related bibliophilic treasures for his library.[7] But his most conspicuous tribute is undoubtedly the 'Shakespeare Recess' created in 1829, a shrine to the writer visible from the stairs of the Museum (Fig.1). It was not England's first architectural alignment of Shakespeare with religious beliefs past and present: in 1740 a monument to his memory, designed by William Kent, was erected in Westminster Abbey, while David Garrick used the grounds of his house in Twickenham as the setting for a temple housing a statue of Shakespeare by Louis-François Roubiliac (Fig.2).[8] Kent's memorial co-opted Shakespeare into the Anglican establishment, while Garrick's garden building used the language of classical architecture to align Shakespeare with Greek and Roman deities - proving that Shakespeare was indeed the god of his idolatry.

Soane's exercise in bardolatry is more personal and more subversive than either of these precedents.[9] The bust that dominates the Recess was cast from the monument to Shakespeare in Holy Trinity Church, Stratford-upon-Avon[10]; memorial urges may also govern the choice of a painting on the left wall by Henry Howard, which represents King Lear holding the body of the dead Cordelia (Fig.3). From the *Description of the House and*

Left: Fig. 1 The Shakespeare Recess, Sir John Soane's Museum. Photo: Derry Moore

Fig. 2 Johann Zoffany, *The Temple to Shakespeare at Hampton House with Mr and Mrs Garrick,* 1762, G1119, courtesy of the Garrick Club

Museum on the North Side of Lincoln's Inn Fields (1835), we know that this painting specifically illustrates the lines spoken by Lear: 'Howl, howl, howl, howl! O, you are men of stones. / Had I your tongues and eyes, I'd use them so / That heaven's vault should crack. She's gone for ever.'[11]

There are a number of possible personal resonances here for Soane, who would certainly have endorsed Lear's sentiment, 'Sharper than a serpent's tooth it is / To have a thankless child', given his belief that the unkindness of his son George had brought about his wife Eliza's death.[12] The choice of this particular passage from Shakespeare's play may, indeed, be Soane's oblique elegy to his wife, from whose death in 1815 Soane never fully recovered.[13] *King Lear* is a play that has often been read as anticipating atheism in its exclamations against the cruelty of the gods, and its representation of death as final.[14] Perhaps this spoke

to Soane; within the context he created, the scene may question the Christian hope of resurrection but resoundingly suggests the cathartic and immortalising value of Shakespeare's art.[15]

The Recess draws on conventional religious pieties too. Soane, who made sophisticated and ironic use of Catholic iconography elsewhere in the Museum, would surely have noted that - even allowing for the fact that the sexes are reversed - Howard's painting recalls a *pietà*, the image of Mary holding the body of the dead Christ.[16] The Recess features other ecclesiastical references in the window on the east side, an assemblage of stained glass fragments with religious subject-matter: the Annunciation, the Prodigal Son, the Raising of Lazarus, the Last Supper, St Peter, St Paul, St Andrew and St Matthias.[17] Here and elsewhere, Soane exploited the dramatic effects that stained glass could create; the 1832 *Description* of the house

Fig. 3 Henry Howard, *Lear and Cordelia*, 1820, SM P212

mentions that much of the stained glass in the Soane Museum was taken from churches and monasteries during the French Revolution, which seems a likely source for this particular glass.[18]

The cherubim surrounding the ceiling are a standard ornament in baroque churches, and seem decorously in keeping with the glass - until one notices the Phrygian caps that they are wearing (Fig.4).[19] This style of headgear would have signified liberty and radicalism to anyone of Soane's generation, given its associations with the French Revolution. Here it makes a cryptic statement: perhaps poking fun at conventional religion, certainly liberating the cherubim from their usual Judaeo-Christian associations.[20] The intention may be to redeploy the cherubim in the cause of untrammelled fancy and imagination, gesturing towards the wider notion of the supernatural in Shakespeare's dramatic work.

If so, this would resonate with the larger of the two paintings in the Recess, Henry Howard's *The Vision of Shakespeare* (Fig.5). Specially commissioned by Soane, this is an allegorical tribute to Shakespeare's genius, depicting a selection of characters from his plays and showing him in command of the Muses.[21] To quote from the 1835 *Description*, it

> represents the bard resting on the lap of Fancy, contemplating the "visions of glory" which she invokes, while Lyrical Poetry, rising from the earth, invites him to ascend the brightest heaven of invention.[22] Tragedy and Comedy are calling before him the shadowy forms of his principal dramatic characters: near him, Titania, watched by Oberon, is sleeping in her bower, and a train of fairies are sporting about him; on one side, the stars are shooting from their spheres

"to hear the sea-maid's music;" [23] on the other side is the Tempest, the enchanted isle, and its inhabitants; above is Hecate riding on a cloud; and Genii, the offspring of Fancy, are hovering near her sweetest child. [24]

This focus on Shakespeare's magical and supernatural dramas - *A Midsummer Night's Dream*, *Macbeth*, *The Tempest* - continues within another picture which hung in the Recess in Soane's time: Maria Denman's drawing of John Flaxman's bas-relief for Covent Garden Theatre, depicting Shakespeare's role in modern drama (Fig.6). [25] Led by Hecate in a chariot drawn by oxen, the procession in this frieze comprises Macbeth and Lady Macbeth, followed by a cluster of characters from *The Tempest*: Prospero, Miranda, Ferdinand, Ariel and Caliban. Shakespeare brings up the rear, and as a contemporary observer wrote, his 'right arm is extended as in the act of calling up some of the most remarkable personages of the drama'. [26] Eliciting comparisons with Prospero on the one hand and Hecate on the other, Shakespeare is celebrated as the arch-magus of invention.

The Shakespearean paintings placed in other parts of the Museum are inspired by a variety of literary genres and do full justice to the range of Shakespeare's work. [27] In that context, the narrow focus on Shakespeare's supernatural characters in the Recess is striking, and functions above all as a celebration of Shakespeare's visionary qualities. The notion of Shakespeare as the supreme poet of fancy and imagination is very common at this date among Romantic writers, and clearly had implications for admirers working in the very different medium of architecture.

Allied notions of memory dominate a supplementary account of the recess in the *Description* of the museum quoted above, written by Soane's friend Barbara Hofland, and typical of early 19th-century guidebooks in suggesting, even dictating, emotions appropriate to the place. [28]

> We next stop at the recess consecrated to [Shakespeare's] memory, and there cease to smile, though we are not called upon to sigh; for veneration of his stupendous genius, and "thick-coming memories" of all that he has taught us to

Left: Fig. 4 Detail of the cherubs in the Shakespeare Recess. Photo: John Bridges

feel and to know, "possess us wholly." [29] Before our eyes is a cast from that monument which calls itself "the true effigies of William Shakespeare". We have seen many portraits of him, and think that a head more calculated to convey the idea of mental power – features more expressive of benevolence, penetration, and energy – than those of our great poet, will scarcely be found in any actual representation of human nature, at that period of life when he was removed from the world he adorned. Every thing in this recess is in keeping with the sentiment inspired, of honouring the memory and increasing the fame of Shakespeare. The beautiful paintings by Howard ..., the window of ancient paintings, and the cherubs surrounding the ceiling, render it altogether a shrine worthy of him whose glorious name it bears, and whose benign countenance "With courteous action, / Dismisses us to more removed ground." [30]

This Shakespearian quotation comes from the point in *Hamlet* where the Ghost of Hamlet's father seeks private discourse with his son, and the soldier Marcellus comments, 'Look with what courteous action / It wafts you to a more removèd ground'. [31]

The Recess could itself be described as 'more removèd ground'; it is built to be semi-private, both warding one off and inviting one in. Like the Soane Museum as a whole, it functions both as a resource for the formation of public taste, as a deeply personal statement and as a site for initiation. Gregory Dart has commented: 'it is perhaps not too fanciful to think of the Soane Museum ... as ... offering a teasing, covert invitation into the "higher truths" of nature'. [32] Certainly, Soane was a Freemason, like many other architects of his time, and did once stage a ceremony in the Museum which was not unlike an initiation rite. [33] When he acquired one of the highlights of his collection, the Belzoni sarcophagus, he mounted a three-day celebration involving lamp-lit tours of the museum, which his friend James Christie compared to the similarly illuminated mysteries of Eleusis. [34] Hofland's account of the occasion makes insistent reference to the Shakespearian supernatural [35]:

> Had any one of that gay company been placed *alone* in the sepulchral chamber, at the "witching hour of night," when "Churchyards yawn, and graves give up their dead," when the flickering

lights become self-extinguished, and the last murmuring sounds from without ceased to speak of the living world, - it is probable that even the healthiest pulse would have been affected with the darker train of emotions which a situation so unallied to common life is calculated to produce. The awe ameliorated by beauty, and softened by tender reminiscence, would be exchanged for the mysterious expectation of some terrific visitant from the invisible world; and the very strongest mind would explain with Hamlet - "There are more things in heaven and earth, Horatio, / Than are dreamt of in your philosophy".

Strikingly, even though this *seance* was inspired by a piece of Egyptian antiquity, its effect on viewers is described in terms taken from *Hamlet*. In the passage above, not one, but two passages from the play are loosely quoted: Hamlet's famous admission of supernatural belief, and his later comment "Tis now the very witching time of night, / When churchyards yawn, and hell itself breathes out / Contagion to this world'.[36] Sharpening up reference to the sarcophagus, there is also outside interference from Calpurnia's line in *Julius Caesar*: 'graves have yawned and yielded up their dead'.[37]

Though the Soane Museum was left to the British nation as a public resource, it also proffered initiation of a more mystical kind for the well-disposed neophyte. Shakespeare, as Soane's foremost literary hero, has a dominating presence in this. Placing such a personal quasi-religious installation as the Shakespeare Recess in a house-museum intended to educate the general public was a bold statement of Soane's veneration for Shakespeare, at once secularising and mystical. Soane would not have known the actual term 'bardolatry', coined by George Bernard Shaw in the early 20th century, but he helped create the aesthetic that gave birth to it.[38]

Alison Shell is a Professor in the Department of English, University College London.

Above: Fig. 6 Maria Denman, Bas relief by John Flaxman on the front of Covent Garden Theatre representing the Modern Drama, SM P214

Opposite page: Fig. 5 Henry Howard, *The Vision of Shakespeare*, 1830, SM P213

Endnotes

1   I am grateful to Stephanie Coane, Greg Dart, Helen Dorey, Arnold Hunt, Sue Palmer, Andrew Rudd, Frances Sands, Robin Simon and Jo Tinworth for help received at various times during the composition of this essay.

2   M. Dobson, *The Making of the National Poet: Shakespeare, Adaptation and Authorship, 1660-1769*, 1992; J. Bate, *Shakespearean Constitutions: Politics, Theatre, Criticism, 1730-1830*, 1989.

3   *An Ode upon Dedicating a Building and Erecting a Statue, to Shakespeare, at Stratford Upon Avon* (1769), reprinted in B. Vickers (ed.), *William Shakespeare: The Critical Heritage*, vol.5, 1979: repr. 2000, p.345. This alludes to *Romeo and Juliet*, Act 2, Scene 1, lines 154-156. In the original, Juliet says to Romeo, 'Do not swear at all, / Or if thou wilt, swear by thy gracious self, / Which is the god of my idolatry'. See J. Shapiro, *Contested Will: Who Wrote Shakespeare?*, 2010: this ed. 2011, p.33.

4   On bardolatry, see G. Holderness (ed.), *The Shakespeare Myth*, 1988, esp. preface and ch.1; J. Martineau, 'Bardolatry', in *Shakespeare in Art*, ed. Martineau, 2003, pp. 201-215; and G. Taylor, *Reinventing Shakespeare*, 1989, esp. chs 2-3.

5   See F. Macé de Lépinay, *Peintures et Sculptures du Panthéon*, 1997.

6   See H. Dorey, 'Death and Memory: The Architecture of Legacy in Sir John Soane's Museum', in *Death and Memory: Soane and the Architecture of Legacy*, 2015, pp. 7-15, and E. A. Fay, *Fashioning Faces: The Portraitive Mode in British Romanticism*, 2010, p.186. Examples include John Flaxman, bust of William Pitt the younger, Sir John Soane's Museum (hereafter SM), museum

number SC24; gold mourning ring containing a lock of Napoleon's hair, SM X1310. The inscription on the ring, 'Prier pour moi', recalls the Catholic cult of saints' relics.

7   See Stephanie Coane's essay in this volume, pp. 29-37.

8   P. Connell, 'Death and the Author: Westminster Abbey and the Meanings of the Literary Monument', *18th-Century Studies*, 2005, pp. 557-585. See the Twickenham Museum website (www.twickenham-museum.org.uk) for an account of Garrick's villa and the Shakespeare Temple. On Zoffany's painting of the Temple, acquired recently by the Garrick Club, see M. Webster, *Johann Zoffany, 1733-1810*, 2011, ch.4.

9   The arrangement of paintings and objects in the Recess differed at various points during Soane's lifetime and subsequently; see H. Dorey, 'The Shakespeare Recess', unpublished research report, SM. Except where otherwise indicated, the following analysis is based on the details given in Soane's 1835 *Description* of his house and museum.

10   SM SC18. John Britton's privately printed *Remarks on the Life and Writings of William Shakespeare*, 1814, pp. 23-24, calls the bust 'indubitably the most authentic and probable likeness of the poet'.

11   *Description*, p.56; *The Tragedy of King Lear*, Act 5, Scene 3, lines 232-234.

12   *Tragedy of King Lear*, Act 1, Scene 4, lines 268-269. Gillian Darley has commented that *King Lear* 'evoked for Soane the tragedy of his own life, a man almost destroyed by the acts of his own children': *John Soane: An Accidental Romantic*, 1999, p.275. *King Lear*, which had not been

performed in public during George III's final unstable years, was staged again in 1820: Darley, *Soane*, pp. 261-262.

13   SM P212. Soane had purchased the painting - which he may also have commissioned - in 1820, after Eliza's death but some years before the Recess was built: see its entry in the Soane Museum online catalogue http://collections.soane.org.

14   E.g. in W. R. Elton, *'King Lear' and the Gods*, 1966. This was an insight more available to readers than to playgoers in Soane's time. Nahum Tate's version of Shakespeare, which allows Cordelia to live, was standard theatrical fare till 1838: see E. Mullin, 'Macready's Triumph: The Restoration of *King Lear* to the British Stage', *Penn History Review*, 2010, pp. 17-35.

15   On the aesthetic implications of the Shakespeare Recess, see A. Rudd, 'John Soane, Shakespeare and the Eighteenth-Century Style Wars', in K. Halsey and A. Vine (eds), *Shakespeare and Authority*, forthcoming 2017. My thanks to Dr Rudd for letting me see a copy of this before publication.

16   On Soane's alter ego, 'Padre Giovanni', and the Monk's Parlour, see Darley, *Soane*, p.308. On Lear and the *pietà*, see K. Goodland, *Female Mourning and Tragedy in Medieval and Renaissance English Drama*, 2005, ch.8.

17   *Description* (1835), p.57, and Helen Dorey '"Exquisite hues and magical effects": Sir John Soane's use of stained glass at Lincoln's Inn Fields' and 'The History of the installations of stained glass at 13 Lincoln's Inn Fields since Sir John Soane's death in 1837' pp. 7-36 and 41-89 in *The Journal of Stained Glass*, special issue, 2004, at pp. 21 and

58-59. Though the arrangement of stained glass fragments has varied during the course of the Recess's history, it has recently been restored to its earliest state. See Dorey, 'Shakespeare Recess'.

18   *Description of the House and Museum on the North Side of Lincoln's Inn Fields* (1832), p.24.

19   It is not clear whether these would have been specially commissioned by Soane or cast from a pre-existent prototype: see SM, archive bill XV.K.1.5 (my thanks to Helen Dorey for this reference). For another example of cherubs wearing Phrygian caps, see J. Gillray, 'A French Hail Storm' (copy consulted: American Philosophical Society Mss. B. P165). On the various meanings of the Phrygian cap, see J. Epstein, 'Understanding the Cap of Liberty: Symbolic Practice and Social Conflict in Early 19th-Century England', *Past and Present*, 1989, pp. 75-118.

20   Cf. Soane's tomb to Eliza, which eschews Christian imagery: see T. Drysdale, '"With trembling hand this monument he rears": Drawing the Soane Family Tomb', pp. 19-27 in *Death and Memory*, at p. 21.

21   SM P213.

22   This sentence quotes from Thomas Gray's 'The Bard', 'Visions of glory, spare my aching sight!' (line 107: see the digital text in the Thomas Gray Archive, *www.thomasgray.org.uk*) and alludes to the Chorus's opening lines to Shakespeare's *Henry V*: 'O for a muse of fire, that would ascend / The brightest heaven of invention' (Prologue, lines 1-2).

23   *A Midsummer Night's Dream*, Act 2, Scene 1, line 154.

24   *Description* (1835), p.56.

25   *Description* (1835), pp. 56-57; SM P214. See also Dorey, 'Shakespeare Recess'. The classical witch-goddess Hecate is not now thought of as a prominent Shakespearian character, but Puck refers to 'we fairies that do run / By the triple Hecate's team' (*A Midsummer Night's Dream*, Act 5, Scene 2, lines 13-14) and performances of *Macbeth* in Soane's time would have included material featuring Hecate, now usually attributed to Thomas Middleton. See the edition of *Macbeth* in *Thomas Middleton: The Collected Works*, ed. G. Taylor and J. Lavagnino, 2007. D. Roy (ed.), *Romantic and Revolutionary Theatre, 1789-1860*, 2009, p.90, gives a description of how Hecate's entrance was staged at the Drury Lane Theatre in 1794.

26   *The English School: A Series of the Most Approved Productions in Painting and Sculpture, Executed by British Artists*, this ed. 1832, vol. III, p.207. On Soane's admiration for Flaxman and relationship with Denman, see H. Dorey's essay in *John Flaxman 1755-1826: Master of the Purest Line*, ed. D. Bindman, 2003, pp. 25-35.

27   See Helen Dorey (ed.), *Shakespeare and Co.: A literary perambulation around Sir John Soane's Museum*, pamphlet available to purchase at the Museum.

28   *Description* (1835), p. 81. See D. Butts, *"Mistress of our tears": A Literary and Bibliographical Study of Barbara Hofland*, 1992, no.54.

29   'Thick-coming memories' rewrites 'thick-coming fancies' (*Macbeth*, Act 5, Scene 3, line 40). 'Possess us wholly' is a quotation from M. Morgann, *An Essay on the Dramatic Character of Falstaff*, 1825, p.73.

30   Britton, *Remarks*, also associates the bust with Hamlet's father's ghost: 'Whatever comes in a "questionable shape" [quoting *Hamlet*, Act 1, Scene 4, line 24] should be seriously and fastidiously investigated' (p.24).

31   *Hamlet*, Act 1, Scene 4, lines 41-42. 'Wafts' follows the Folio text; some editors adopt the wording in the second quarto (Q2), 'waves'. The misquotation here is likely to be deliberate; a bust cannot wave or waft, but its countenance can 'dismiss'. In the early 19th century 'dismiss' was still synonymous with 'send forth' (*Oxford English Dictionary*).

32   *Metropolitan Art and Literature, 1810-1840: Cockney Adventures*, 2012, p.187.

33   D. Watkin, 'Freemasonry and Sir John Soane', *Journal of the Society of Architectural Historians*, 1995, 402-417.

34   Dart, *Metropolitan Art*, p.184. Something of this effect can be glimpsed in the candlelight tours that the Museum still holds regularly.

35   *Description* (1835), p.39.

36   *Hamlet*, Act 1, Scene 5, lines 168-169 ('our philosophy' in Folio), and Act 3, Scene 2, lines 377-379.

37   *Julius Caesar*, Act 2, Scene 2, line 18. There is also a reference to this episode in *Hamlet*: 'A little ere the mightiest Julius fell, / The graves stood tenantless, and the sheeted dead / Did squeak and gibber in the Roman streets' (Additional passage from Q2, Act 1, Scene 1, 7-9).

38   'Preface to *Three Plays for Puritans*' in *Collected Plays with their Prefaces*, ed. D. H. Laurence, 1971, vol.2, p.41.

Mr. WILLIAM
SHAKESPEARES

COMEDIES,
HISTORIES, &
TRAGEDIES.

Published according to the True Originall Copies.

artin Droeshout sculpsit London.

LONDON

Printed by Isaac Iaggard, and Ed. Blount. 1623.

'My library was dukedom large enough'[1]: Shakespeare in Sir John Soane's library[2]

Stephanie Coane

Sir John Soane's lifetime encompassed a period in which shifts in taste led to the revival of interest in Shakespeare and the consolidation of his cultural status as the embodiment of English literary genius. As the age of 'bardolatry' progressed, themes drawn from Shakespeare permeated the arts, from history painting to architecture to music. As illustrated in other essays in this catalogue, the theme of Shakespeare pervades Soane's house at 13 Lincoln's Inn Fields, most obviously in his creation of the Shakespeare Recess and his commissions for several paintings on Shakespearean themes. He and his family were keen lifelong theatre goers who saw some of the leading performers of the day including Sarah Siddons and her brother John Philip Kemble[3]; and Soane's younger son George incurred parental disapproval in his preference for a career as a writer in theatrical circles rather than paternally approved architectural studies, and in his marriage to the daughter of a now obscure playwright and Shakespearean scholar, James Boaden.[4] The Soanes also visited Shakespeare's birthplace and tomb in Stratford-upon-Avon in August 1810.[5]

Although he is now remembered principally as an architect and collector of arts and antiquities, Soane's library of nearly seven thousand volumes is one of the richest of its time, a unique survival both as the only known professional library of a practising architect of the early nineteenth century, and as a gentleman's town library of the period, essentially unabridged and undiluted, frozen in time at the date of his death, in the book-presses he designed to house it. Even more unusual is the survival of records in his archive, which often enable the identification of the processes by which many of the books were acquired. Soane's library was simultaneously a means of intellectual and social self-improvement, enabling him to rise above his humble origins as a bricklayer's son, and to emulate both the leaders of his profession – men like William Chambers, George Dance, and Robert Adam – and eminent clients such as his first patron the Bishop of Derry, Philip Yorke, 3rd Earl of Hardwicke, and William Beckford.[6] Books from the libraries of all these men and many others he admired were to find a home on Soane's shelves, and so, unsurprisingly, did books by Shakespeare: no fewer than eleven editions of the collected works or collected plays including a copy of the iconic First Folio (Fig.1), the last addition to his library being an illustrated small-format duodecimo edition (mostly unopened) purchased directly from the publisher only a few years before Soane's death in January 1837.[7]

Left: Fig. 1 Title page of Soane's copy of Shakespeare's First Folio

They are supplemented by a handful of secondary works, biographies of actors, and miscellaneous Shakespeareana.

As a young man, John Soane had copied extracts from Shakespeare in his commonplace book[8], and throughout his life, William Dodd's immensely popular anthology *The Beauties of Shakespeare*, which ran through at least 39 editions between 1752 and 1893 despite its compiler's conviction and subsequent hanging for forgery, was a evidently a favourite gift. Two copies survive in his library: that of the 1780 edition may be the one purchased on 13 July 1784, the day after he confided in his notebook that he had cancelled his will and codicils some five weeks before his marriage[9]; that of the 1810 edition is inscribed as the gift of the bookseller James Asperne on 23 February 1813. Records survive of at least four other copies: one from Asperne on 28 April 1814[10], another 'ordered for Miss P[atterson] as a present for her kindness in making the Catalogue of my Library' on 16 April 1815[11], another bought from Asperne in July 1817[12], and yet another from his printer, James Moyes, on 28 May 1822.[13]

Soane's earliest datable purchase of a work by Shakespeare is a copy of *Othello* "… as it is now acted at the Theatres Royal in Drury-Lane and Covent-Garden" printed in 1765.[14] Bound in a collection of plays by Sir John Vanbrugh and others dated between 1760 and 1770, its frontispiece, inscribed 'J Soan', indicates it was in his possession before he altered the spelling of his name in 1784 (another similar collection of plays by Susanna Centlivre and Vanbrugh bears the same inscription dated 1777).[15] His enthusiastic appetite for Shakespeare, however, was first stimulated by Alderman John Boydell's immensely popular Shakespeare Gallery, which opened on Pall Mall in May 1789 (see p.12) with the ostensible aim of founding a British school of history painting, supported by the commercial goal of selling engravings of the paintings. Boydell spent a fortune on his Shakespeare project, commissioning 167 paintings by the leading artists of the day and issuing a collection of 96 large engravings, eventually published complete in two elephant folio volumes dated 1803, and an illustrated edition of *The dramatic works of Shakspeare* in nine folio volumes dated 1802 featuring reduced versions of the engravings, a copy of which is in Soane's library. By late 1803, the Gallery was in financial difficulties as a result of overgenerous commissions, problems with the quality of the engravings, and the effect of the French wars on trade generally, and Boydell applied to Parliament for leave to conduct a lottery to raise money by disposing of the Gallery and its contents; he died before the lottery (of which Soane was a trustee)[16] could be drawn, and the pictures were later sold at Christie's, 17-20 May 1805.[17] Soane acquired two of the paintings, William Hamilton's *The Landing of Richard II at Milford Haven* (Fig.2) and a large scene of Falstaff in disguise from *The Merry Wives of Windsor* by James Durno (see p.14).[18]

Many of Soane's early book purchases were aimed at building the professional library of a working architect, a process greatly aided by the death of his wife Eliza's wealthy uncle George Wyatt in 1790, leaving her a substantial inheritance. Two years later Soane acquired the freehold of 12 Lincoln's Inn Fields, which he rebuilt as a home for his growing family, and equipped with an architectural office and library to house his book collection for his own and his apprentices' edification.[19] The years between 1800 and 1809 saw two further reasons for the substantial increase in Soane's book buying: his purchase in August 1800 of Pitzhanger Manor in Ealing, which he rebuilt with its own country house library to create an artistic environment to educate his sons as architects[20]; and his appointment on 28 March 1806 as Professor of Architecture at the Royal Academy, for which he had already begun to prepare by embarking on an ambitious programme of reading and note-taking. Soane's Royal Academy lectures are sprinkled with quotations (and misquotations) from Shakespeare[21], and it seems likely that his first datable purchase of the collected plays, an 1803 reprint of 'Mr. Steevens's last edition' (i.e. the fourth edition of Shakespeare's works as edited by Samuel Johnson and George Steevens, published in 1793), bought in boards from the publisher Robert Scholey on 25 July 1806, was stimulated by the need for a working copy of more manageable proportions than the Boydell folios.[22] This set was later rebound uniformly with a copy of *An index to the remarkable passages and words made use of by Shakspeare* (1790), compiled by Samuel Ayscough, which may have been acquired at the same time to aid the discovery of suitable passages, as may the copy of Francis Twiss, *A complete verbal index to the plays of Shakspeare* (1805), although neither can be dated from archival evidence.[23]

By 1809 Soane was obliged to admit failure as far as his sons' architectural future was concerned, and in July 1810 he sold Pitzhanger and amalgamated the two collections at Lincoln's Inn Fields, taking up residence in the larger house he had rebuilt next door at No.13 to accommodate his growing museum and library in 1813. From the early 1820s a change can be discerned in his book buying. His bitter estrangement from his younger son George in late 1815, following the publication of the latter's vicious attacks on his father in the press and the death of Eliza Soane, was followed by the premature death of his older son John junior in October 1823. Alongside these private disappointments came growing public approbation of his collection, exemplified by a description in the *Morning Chronicle* on 20 March 1821:

> The Library is stored with almost every known work in Architecture; no expence has been spared in procuring the most scarce and useful, as well as the most splendid publications. ... The united collection is perhaps unrivalled, considered as belonging to an individual Artist, and the result of his increasing application, talent, taste, and liberality.[24]

Although Soane was by now having trouble with his eyesight, suspending his Royal Academy lectures and employing assistants to read to him in the evenings, it is in the 1820s that the greatest bibliophile's treasures in his library were acquired. Chief among these are the copies of the four seventeenth-century folios of the collected plays of Shakespeare, and most especially the celebrated First Folio of 1623.

When the First Folio was published seven years after Shakespeare's death, its editors (Shakespeare's fellow actors and friends, John Heminge and Henry Condell) could have had little notion that it would become one of the most sought-after books in any collector's library. Shakespeare's reputation as the greatest writer in the English language was slow to develop. The Folio was reprinted in 1632, 1663 and 1685 (the Second, Third, and Fourth Folios), but as fashions changed his plays were performed less frequently, and then usually in heavily adapted forms: even David Garrick retained Nahum Tate's happy ending for King Lear.[25] Most early eighteenth-century editions merely marked up the text of the previous edition, correcting or regularising spelling and punctuation but also introducing errors of their own or imposing their own principles of taste or metre, as in Alexander Pope's

Fig. 2 William Hamilton, *The Landing of Richard II at Milford Haven, c.*1793-1800, SM P147

edition and later editions based on it, for example that of Thomas Hanmer, whose handsome typography and fine engravings by Hubert Gravelot after Francis Hayman (the 1771 Oxford edition of which is in Soane's library) do not make up for the infelicities of its editorial approach.[26] By the mid-eighteenth century, however, with the Shakespeare revival in full swing and engravings of Hogarth's portrait of Garrick as Richard III flying off the presses, editors such as Samuel Johnson, Edward Capell, and Edmond Malone (all represented in Soane's library) began to recognise the importance of returning as closely as possible to the earliest reliable texts of each play, and the First Folio, without which eighteen of Shakespeare's best loved plays (*Macbeth, Twelfth Night,* and *The Tempest* to name a few) might well have been lost to us, took its place at the pinnacle of the book collector's canon. The turn of the eighteenth to nineteenth centuries was the age of 'bibliomania', to use the word coined by Soane's

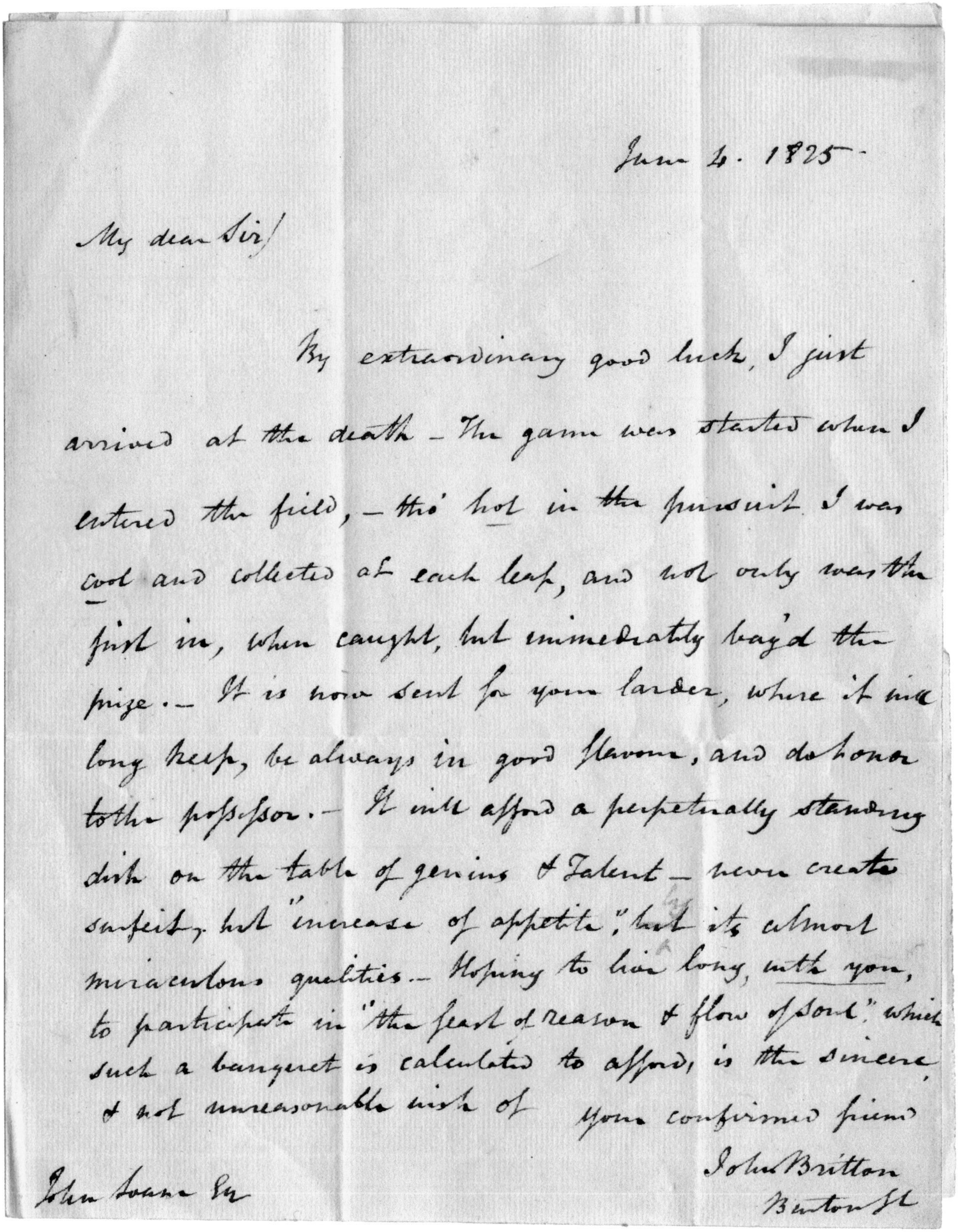

Jun. 4. 1825.

My dear Sir,

By extraordinary good luck, I just arrived at the death – The game was started when I entered the field, – tho' hot in the pursuit. I was cool and collected at each leap, and not only was the first in, when caught, but immediately bag'd the prize. – It is now sent for your larder, where it will long keep, be always in good flavour, and do honor to the possessor. – It will afford a perpetually standing dish on the table of genius & Talent – never create surfeit, but "increase of appetite", but its almost miraculous qualities. – Hoping to live long, with you, to participate in "the feast of reason & flow of soul" which such a banquet is calculated to afford, is the sincere, & not unreasonable wish of

your confirmed friend
John Britton
Burton St

John Soane Esq

Fig. 3 Letter from John Britton to Soane describing his purchase
of Shakespeare's First Folio on his behalf

acquaintance, the bibliophile Thomas Frognall Dibdin, and prices of the First Folio rose vertiginously.[27]

Soane's copy of the First Folio was acquired on his behalf by his friend the antiquarian and Shakespeare enthusiast John Britton on 24 May 1825 for the large sum of £105 at the sale of library of James Boswell the younger, editor of the 1821 'Third Variorum' edition of the works of Shakespeare, itself bought by Soane on 28 February 1822, and now considered the foundation of modern Shakespeare scholarship.[28] Britton wrote to Soane on 4 June (Fig.3) to announce his success, employing the over-extended metaphor of a stag hunt:

> My Dear Sir, By extraordinary good luck I just arrived at the death – The game was started when I entered the field, – though hot in the pursuit, I was cool and collected at each leap, and not only was the first when caught, but immediately bag'd the prize. – It is now sent for your larder, where it will long keep, be always in good flavour, and do honor to the possessor. – It will afford a perpetual standing dish, on the table of genius & Talent - never create surfeit, but "increase of appetite" [by] its almost miraculous qualities. – Hoping to live long, with you, to participate in "the feast of reason & the flow of soul", which such a banquet is calculated to afford, is the sincere & not unreasonable wish of Your confirmed friend John Britton.[29]

An additional attraction for Soane was the provenance of this copy, which Boswell had bought at the sale of the library of John Philip Kemble, the leading actor of the day, whose portrait in the role of Coriolanus hangs in Soane's Picture Room Recess (see p.45).[30] Boswell's rueful comment after laying out the then astonishing sum of £112.7.0, quoted by Dibdin in his account of First Folio price inflation, must have resonated with Soane: 'It has become still more expensive. *Ipse miserrimus* gave a much larger sum at Mr. Kemble's sale; but I could not bring myself to a cold calculation of the value of a copy which was at once a memorial of Shakespeare and of Kemble.'[31] Boswell's sensibility would have been shared by Soane, for whom 'the idea behind a book or an object, the story that it told, and the connections and associations that it set off in his mind through its content or its previous owners were at least as important as its physical appearance or monetary value'.[32] Although believed by Dibdin to have been commissioned by Boswell, it is all but certain that the sumptuous binding of gold-tooled olive green straight-grained morocco by John Mackinlay (Fig.4) with the leaves 'washed white and clean and inlaid in consequence of the edges having been cut very close'[33] was undertaken for Kemble, as the 1821 sale catalogue describes his First Folio as a 'very fine copy, most carefully inlaid throughout bound in Venetian morocco'.[34]

It is not known when or where Soane acquired his copies of the Second, Third, and Fourth Folios[35], but there is no evidence to support Soane's later assertion that all four Folios had belonged to Kemble[36]; nor is it known when and where he acquired possibly the rarest edition of a work by Shakespeare in his library, a copy of the second quarto issue of *Henry IV, Part 1*.[37] However, Kemble's First Folio joined another Shakespeare edition with a glittering theatrical provenance: David Garrick's copy of George Steevens's 1766 edition of *Twenty of the plays of Shakespeare*. Steevens was the first editor since the publication of the First Folio to study the early quarto editions of the plays in order to establish more accurate versions of the original texts.[38] Soane's set is probably the finest in existence, being one of twelve copies printed on fine paper, bound in contemporary gold-tooled red morocco (Fig.5) for presentation to Garrick by Steevens, who had consulted copies of the original quartos in the actor's extensive library; Soane, already the owner of a set of the ordinary paper issue received as a gift in 1821,[39] bought it on 3 May 1823 for £25.4.0 plus commission from the booksellers T. & W. Boone following the Garrick sale on 23 April.[40]

Perhaps the oddest Shakespearean curiosity in Soane's library is the copy of William Henry Ireland's notorious *Miscellaneous papers and legal instruments under the hand and seal of William Shakspeare*. Published by his father Samuel Ireland in 1796, the book purported to contain transcripts of rediscovered documents in Shakespeare's hand; the 'discovery' briefly generated bardolatrous veneration before being swiftly and conclusively unmasked as forgeries by the scholar Edmond Malone.[41] Soane's copy of the book, bought thirty years after the events on 13 November 1826, includes scribal copies of some of the documents together with critical remarks in a scholarly hand.[42] It seems fitting that Soane's library should contain both extremes of the age of bardolatry.

Dr Stephanie Coane is Senior Librarian, College Library, Eton College and Honorary Librarian to Sir John Soane's Museum.

Far left: Fig. 4 The olive green morocco binding of Soane's copy of Shakespeare's First Folio

Left: Fig. 5 The handsome red morocco binding of one of the volumes of David Garrick's copy of George Steevens's 1766 edition of *Twenty of the plays of Shakespeare*

Endnotes

1   *The Tempest*, Act 1, Scene 2, lines 109-110.

2   I am especially grateful to Sue Palmer and Alison Shell for assistance received during the composition of this essay; and to all those whose help and advice contributed to the recent completion of the online catalogue of Soane's library, most notably Stephen Astley, Eileen Harris, Stephen Massil, Sue Palmer, and Nicholas Savage. The catalogue can be accessed at http://collections.soane.org/books.

3   See Helen Dorey's essay 'Soane as a collector', in Peter Thornton and Helen Dorey, *A miscellany of objects from Sir John Soane's Museum*, 1992, pp. 123-4.

4   Gillian Darley, *John Soane: an accidental Romantic*, 1999, pp. 201, 204-208.

5   Ibid., p. 198. The copy of a guidebook by Robert Wheler Bell, *History and antiquities of Stratford-upon-Avon* (1806), was presumably acquired for the occasion.

6   Eileen Harris, 'Sir John Soane's library: "O books! Ye monuments of mind"', *Apollo*, Apr. 1990, p. 242.

7   *The plays and poems of Shakspeare, … in fifteen volumes* (London: A.J. Valpy, 1832-1834). A draft of a note from Soane to Valpy dated 4 January 1834 requesting another copy of vol. 4, 'the former one having been stolen from him', survives in Soane's personal archive (SM Archive, Priv. Corr. XVI.F.123).

8   Soane Case 139.

9   Darley, op. cit., p. 75.

10 SM Archive, Spiers Box, Loose Bills.

11 SM Archive, 4/B/7/3.

12 Guildhall Library, Trades File, entry for James Asperne covering transactions between Soane and Asperne for the period 1814-1817.

13 SM Archive, Priv. Corr. XVI.E.4.1.

14 Such texts were usually ephemeral, being issued as souvenirs of particular performances, and often varied not inconsiderably from Shakespeare's text (most notoriously in the case of Nahum Tate's adaptation of King Lear, with its happy ending for Edgar and Cordelia, which continued to be performed as late as 1838). See Stanley Wells, *Shakespeare for all time*, 2002, pp. 191-3, 198.

15 No works by Shakespeare appear in the manuscript list of Soane's library *c*.1782, in his 'Notes Italy and Italian Language' (SM Vol. 162), pp. 291-287; reproduced in Pierre de la Ruffinière Du Prey, *John Soane's architectural education* (PhD thesis, 1972), appendix B, pp. 354-363.

16 SM Archive, Priv. Corr. V.I.11.1-2.

17 See Robin Hamlyn, 'The Shakespeare Galleries of John Boydell and James Woodmason', in Jane Martineau et al., *Shakespeare in art*, 2003, pp. 97-101; Wells, op. cit., pp. 241-244.

18 SM P147; SM P211.

19 Harris, op. cit., p. 242; Darley, op. cit., pp. 97-100.

20 See Darley, op. cit., ch. 9.

21 See index to David Watkin, *Sir John Soane: Enlightenment thought and the Royal Academy Lectures*, 1996.

22 SM Archive, 16/12/34.

23 SM Archive, 7/14/36.

24 *Morning Chronicle*, 20 March 1821, quoted in Harris, op. cit., p. 246.

25 Stanley Wells, op.cit., pp. 191-193, 216.

26 Ibid., pp. 202-4.

27 A. J. West, *The Shakespeare First Folio: the history of the book. Vol. 1. An account of the First Folio based on its sale and prices, 1623-2000*, 2001, pp. 87-88 and 90-97.

28 SM Archive, Priv. Corr. XVI.E.4.8.

29 ALs housed with the copy of the First Folio.

30 SM, P99.

31 Thomas Frognall Dibdin, *The library companion*, 1824, p. 792.

32 Nicholas Savage, 'Hooked on books: interpreting Sir John Soane's library', *The Private Library*, 5th ser., vol. 10:1 (Spring 2007), p. 50.

33 Dibdin, op. cit., p. 808.

34 R. H. Evans, *A catalogue of the … library, choice prints, and theatrical portraits, of John Philip Kemble Esq.*, 1821, no. 1657*.

35 See Appendix for details.

36 Sir John Soane, *Description of the house and museum on the north side of Lincoln's Inn Fields, the residence of Sir John Soane*, 1835, p. 8.

37 *The historie of Henry the Fourth: vvith the battell at Shrewesbury, betweene the King, and Lord Henry Percy, surnamed Henry Hotspur of the north. With the humorous conceits of Sir Iohn Falstaffe* (London: printed by Iohn Norton, and are to bee sold by William Sheares, 1632).

38 Eileen Harris and Nicholas Savage, *Hooked on books: the library of Sir John Soane, architect, 1753-1837*, exh. cat., 2004, pp. 29-30.

39 Soane's notebook for 27 March 1821 records a copy brought 'as a Present by Mr. T. [i.e. his friend John Taylor].

40 SM Archive, Priv. Corr. XVI.E.5.5.

41 Edmond Malone, *An inquiry into the authenticity of certain miscellaneous papers and legal instruments*, 1796; see Wells, op. cit., pp. 272-4.

42 SM Archive, Priv. Corr. XVI.E.6.11.

Appendix

Chronological list of collected editions of Shakespeare in Sir John Soane's library:

Title	Imprint	Date of purchase (where known)	Reference no.
Mr. VVilliam Shakespeares comedies, histories & tragedies. Published from the true originall copies. [THE FIRST FOLIO: with the title-page in the second state with the collar shaded]	London: printed by Isaac Jaggard, and Ed. Blount, 1623	24 May 1825	SM 1526
Mr. William Shakespeares comedies, histories, and tragedies. ... The second impression. [THE SECOND FOLIO: the eighth of nine imprint variants, in fact a remainder from Allot's stock with sheet πA2.5 reset by Cotes some time after 1640, with the title-page imprint partly printed over the engraving]	London: printed by Tho. Cotes, for Robert Allot, 1632		SM 1525
Mr. William Shakespear's comedies, histories, and tragedies. ... The third impression. And unto this impression is added seven playes, never before printed in folio. ... [THE THIRD FOLIO: in the second issue, including seven additional plays]	London: printed [by Roger Daniel, Alice Warren, and another] for P.C. [i.e. Philip Chetwind], 1664		SM 3976
Mr William Shakespear's Comedies, histories, and tragedies. ... The fourth edition. [THE FOURTH FOLIO: one of two title-page settings, and the third of three imprint variants, being a cancel and therefore later]	London: printed for H. Herringman, and are to be sold by Joseph Knight and Francis Saunders, 1685		SM 1527
Twenty of the plays of Shakespeare, being the whole number printed in quarto during his life-time, or before the Restoration, collated where there were different copies, and publish'd from the originals, by George Steevens	London: printed for J. and R. Tonson; T. Payne; and W. Richardson, 1766	Copy 1 (fine paper issue, Garrick's copy): 3 May 1823 Copy 2 (ordinary paper issue): 27 March 1821	SM 1528

Mr William Shakespeare his comedies, histories, and tragedies, set out by himself in quarto, or by the players his friends in folio, and now faithfully republished from those editions … [edited by Edward Capell]	London: printed by Dryden Leach, for J. and R. Tonson, 1768		SM 3677
The works of Shakespear [edited by Sir Thomas Hanmer, with engravings by H. Gravelot after Francis Hayman], 2nd edition	Oxford: printed at the Clarendon Press, 1771		SM 1530
The plays of William Shakespeare. [2nd Johnson & Steevens edition]	London: printed for C. Bathurst, W. Strahan, J.F. and C. Rivington [and 30 others in London], 1778		SM 3679
The dramatic works of Shakspeare. Revised by George Steevens. [First Boydell edition]	London: printed by W. Bulmer & Co., Shakspeare Printing-Office, for John and Josiah Boydell, George & W. Nicol; from the types of W. Martin, 1802		SM 615
The plays of William Shakspeare [reprinted from Johnson and Steevens's 4th edition]	London: printed by T. Bensley; for Wynne and Scholey, and J. Wallis, 1803-5	25 July 1806	SM 3680
The plays and poems of William Shakspeare, with the corrections and illustrations of various commentators [3rd Variorum edition by Boswell and Malone]	London: printed for F.C. and J. Rivington; T. Egerton; J. Cuthell [and 36 others in London, Cambridge, York, and Edinburgh], 1821	28 February 1822	SM 1500
The plays and poems of Shakspeare [reprinted from the 3rd Variorum edition, with illustrations reduced from the plates in the Boydell edition]	London: printed and published by A.J. Valpy, 1832-4	18 October 1832	SM 4665

THEATRE ROYAL, COVENT-GARDEN

This present TUESDAY, May 22, 1821, will be acted Shakspeare's Play of

THE TEMPEST;

Or, The Enchanted Island.

(As altered and adapted by DRYDEN and DAVENANT.)

With additional Musick, new Scenery, Machinery, Dresses, and Decorations.

The Overture composed by Mr. DAVY.

The Original Musick by Purcell—The Additional Musick by Haydn, Mozart, Dr. Arne, Linley, Braham, Mayer, Martini, Paesina, Rossini, &c.

Selected, adapted, and arranged by Mr. BISHOP.

The Scenery painted by Mess Pugh, Grieve, T Grieve, W. Grieve, & assistants.

The Machinery by Mr. EDMUND SAUL.

The Changes, and Decorations by Mr. BRADWELL and Mr. W. BRADWELL.

The Dresses by Mr. Palmer & Miss Egan

Prospero (the rightful Duke of MILAN, a MAGICIAN) by Mr. MACREADY.

Alonzo, King of Naples, by Mr. EGERTON,

Hippolyto, the Duke of Mantua, by Mr. DURUSET,

Antonio, the Usurper of Milan, Mr. CHAPMAN,

Prince Ferdinand of Naples by Mr. ABBOTT,

Gonzalo, a Neapolitan Counsellor, by Mr. JEFFERIES,

Trinculo, the King's Jester, Mr. BLANCHARD,

Stephano, a Sailor of the King's ship, Mr. W. FARREN,

Caliban, a monster of the Island, Mr. EMERY,

Miranda } with Songs, { Miss HALLANDE,
Dorinda } { Miss STEPHENS,

Ariel by Miss FOOTE,

Chorus of Spirits, First Spirit, Mr. PYNE,

Mess. Crumpton, George, Johnson, Montague, Norris, G. Pyne, I. Taylor, S. and C. Tett, Tinney, Watts, Williams, &c. Mesds Appleton, Coates, E Green, Grimald, Herbert, Hibbert, Hudson, Mears, Morris, Parim, Port, Shaw, Watts, &c.

The Dances by

Mess Ba net, Collet, Grant, Heath, Sutton, Vedy.

Mesdames Louis, Wells, S. Shotter, Chipp, Twamley, Vedy, Zara.

After which will be performed, for the first time, a *New Farce (with some Musick,)* called

The Grand Tour;

OR,
STOPPED at ROCHESTER!

The Musick composed by Mr. WARE.

The Scenes painted by Mess. Pugh and Grieve, jun.

The Principal Characters by

Mr. BLANCHARD,
Mr. JONES,
Mr. DURUSET,
Mr. LISTON,
Mr. YATES,
Mr. EMERY,
Mr. CHAPMAN, Mr. CLAREMONT,
Mr. BARNES, Mr. HEATH, Mr. LOUIS,
Mrs. DAVENPORT,
Miss BEAUMONT, Miss SHAW.

☞ All Orders are, for the present, inadmissible.

Printed by E. Macleith, 2, Bow-street.

Shakspeare's Play of The TEMPEST was performed on Saturday to another brilliant and overflowing audience, and received with increased applause—it will be repeated on Thursday and Friday.

In consequence of the demand for Places,

UNDINE; or the SPIRIT of the WATERS,

will be repeated for the 23d and 24th times on Friday and Monday.

Miss DANCE

will perform Tomorrow, LADY TOWNLY.

Tomorrow, the Comedy of The PROVOKED HUSBAND.

On Thursday (5th time) Shakspeare's Play of The TEMPEST.

On Friday, the Play of The TEMPEST

On Saturday will be produced, *for the first time,* a NEW TRAGEDY, called

DAMON and PYTHIAS.

With New Scenery, Dresses and Decorations.

The characters by Mr. MACREADY, Mr. C. KEMBLE, Mr. CHAPMAN, Mr ABBOTT, Mr. EGERTON, Mr COMER, Mr. CONNOR, Mr. JEFFERIES, Mr. MEARS, Miss DANCE, Miss FOOTE, Mrs. CONNOR.

On Tuesday, for the Benefit of the FUND of the Philanthropic Institution, Globe Tavern, the Romance of HENRI QUATRE—with a variety of Songs, and the Farce of TOO LATE FOR DINNER.

At the Play: Soane's experience of Shakespeare in the theatre 1794–1820

Emmeline Leary

Many aspects of attending a Shakespeare play in Soane's time such as the choice of theatre, obtaining a ticket, seating arrangements, the behaviour of the audience and, not least, the presentation of Shakespeare's works were profoundly different from that expected today. Although there was a strong emphasis on contemporary plays, Shakespearean drama continued to hold its place on the stage and Soane attended performances for almost twenty-five years.

For most of the period, only three venues holding a patent to perform spoken drama in London were open during a typical year. Both the Drury Lane and Covent Garden theatres (both a short walk from Lincoln's Inn Fields), operated a season from about September to the following July offering a similar repertoire of Shakespeare, contemporary drama and English comic operas usually performed from Monday to Saturday. In the summer months, only one venue, the Little Theatre on the Haymarket was open. This group was joined by the Lyceum Theatre in 1807.

As schedules of performances were planned just a few days in advance by the theatre management, Soane would only have discovered what was to be performed on any particular night by reading playbills pasted up outside the theatres (Fig.1) or by searching for advertisements in the daily newspapers. Most performances began at 6.30pm which in Soane's time was after dinner, and often lasted for four or more hours as it was usual to present at least two pieces each evening, for example the performance of *Macbeth* attended by Elizabeth Soane on 17 October 1805 was followed by the comedy, *Bon Ton*.

In order to obtain a ticket for all parts of the auditorium apart from the boxes, large numbers, perhaps hundreds of prospective members of the audience had to assemble outside the theatre well in advance of the performance. Boisterous crowds formed by the relevant doors which led to the different seating areas, then at a time which had been advertised in advance (usually an hour before the performance began) they rushed forward to buy tickets at barriers inside the entrances. This part of the procedure was not only an uncomfortable experience but could be dangerous. On one occasion in 1794 it was reported that 15 people had been killed as the crowd rushed forward to buy tickets for a royal command performance at the Little Theatre.

Left: Fig. 1 Playbill for the Theatre Royal, Covent Garden, 22 May 1821. Private collection

Once tickets had been purchased, the crowds poured into the auditorium with the aim of obtaining the best possible seat. This was a crucial moment in the process as the seating (apart from the boxes) consisted of continuous benches and ticket-holders were not allocated a specific place (Fig.2). The main seating areas were the boxes, the pit (now known as the stalls), the gallery and the upper gallery. Ticket prices varied according to the area of the theatre to be occupied. At Drury Lane in the 1814-15 season for example, individual seats in the boxes were seven shillings, tickets for the Pit were 3s 6d, the Gallery 2s and the Upper Gallery 1s. This price structure was intended to reflect the social standing of the audience. As members of the middle-class, John and Elizabeth Soane usually sat in the pit and as can be inferred from the sums recorded as 'expenses of the play' in their notebooks. However, Soane very occasionally paid for a box seat as on 3 July 1815 when he attended a performance of *Richard III* with Edmund Kean in the title role and recorded spending 8s 6d. This sum would have paid for a 7s box seat together with other expenses. At that time, £1 (20 shillings) was worth about £80 in today's currency.

In addition to bench-seating, the appearance of the auditoria differed from those of today, being lit by chandeliers and wall lights which remained illuminated during performances so that members of the audience were visible to each other and to the performers. As a consequence, not only was talking acceptable during performances but loudly expressed responses to the performance, both favourable and unfavourable, were the norm. During the production of *The Tempest* seen by Mrs Soane in December 1806, it was reported that: 'Some persons in the Pit expressed their disapprobation, but their noisy displeasure was soon silenced. This was the only interruption the performance experienced, and the Tempest was announced for a second representation without a dissentient voice.'[1]

Evidence of the theatrical performances attended by John and Elizabeth Soane is found in the notebooks kept by each in which they usually recorded in a few lines the events of each day and the cost of any purchases. However, the information relating to the theatre is limited in that both frequently omitted to give the names of the plays, the theatres they attended as well as their reactions to the performances.

In addition, the notebook sequence for Mrs Soane is incomplete, covering only the period 1804 to 1813 with a gap from late 1807 to the end of 1810. Although it is impossible to be sure that John and Elizabeth Soane recorded every instance of their theatregoing, a broad pattern emerges from the notebooks. It seems that they rarely attended theatrical performances together although *Romeo and Juliet* on 19 October 1807 and *Othello* at Liverpool in the summer of 1810 were two such occasions. Mrs Soane was often accompanied by women friends or her sons. Soane usually went by himself, with men friends or with his sons.

Both John and Elizabeth Soane attended the theatre occasionally rather than regularly: sometimes as infrequently as once a year but taken as a whole, the notebooks reveal that they experienced the full range of theatrical productions available at that time. Alongside drama by Shakespeare they saw major and minor pieces by contemporary playwrights, full-length comic operas in English as well as the annual lavish pantomimes to which they usually took one or both of their sons. Purely musical events such as the oratorios held in the theatres during Lent, Italian opera at the King's Theatre and concerts were also recorded. Despite Elizabeth Soane being away from London in the summer months, her theatre visits were more frequent than her husband's. In 1805 for example, she attended four plays, between January and June and two plays in October. Soane in contrast attended two plays, one in July and the other in November.

It is clear from newspaper advertisements that a greater number of Shakespearean plays were staged during a typical year in London than is the case today. During the 1793-94 season for example, when Soane attended *King Lear*, Covent Garden also offered eight other productions while seven were shown by Drury Lane together with the Little Theatre. This was in addition to the large number of works staged as daily changes of programme rather than long runs of single plays were the norm. Over the period recorded in her notebooks Mrs Soane saw five plays covering a wide range of Shakespeare's work: *The Tempest, Romeo and Juliet, Othello, Macbeth* and *Katharine and Petruchio* (*The Taming of the Shrew*). Soane favoured the tragedies, attending *Othello* three times, *Richard III* and *Macbeth* twice and *Hamlet, King Lear, The Merchant of Venice* and *Romeo and Juliet* once each. He was possibly motivated to

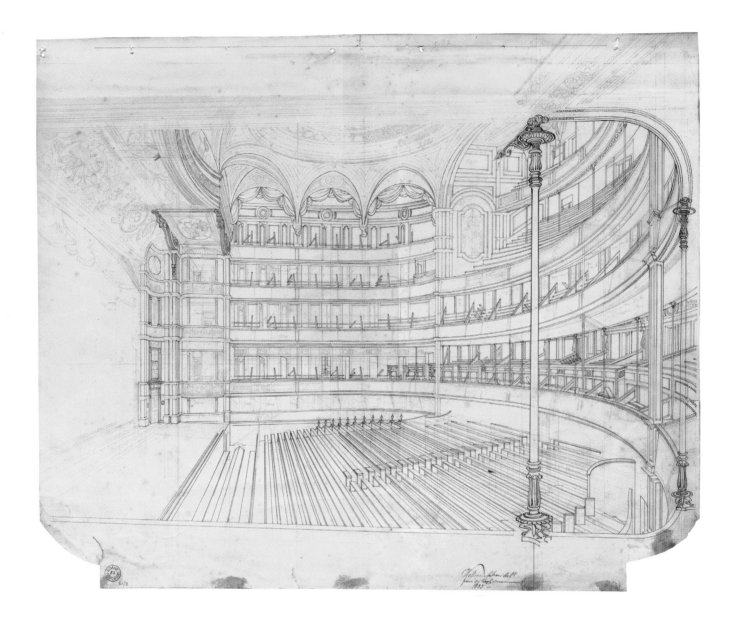

Fig. 2 William Capon, outline perspective
of the interior of the Theatre Royal, Drury
Lane (as rebuilt by Henry Holland), 1805,
SM 61/3/33

select these particular plays as they provided an opportunity to see performances by the leading actors of the time such as John Philip Kemble and Edmund Kean. Soane's notebooks specifically mention Kean in association with four Shakespeare plays, the first being *Richard III* on 5 December 1814. 'Went to see Kean in Richard, the first time.' In addition to those Shakespeare plays specifically named in the notebooks or which can be inferred, others could have been attended, for example on 2 June 1797 when Soane states that the was 'At the play.' On this day *Richard III* was staged at Covent Garden and a non-Shakespearean programme at Drury Lane.

A feature of the theatrical year seldom seen today was the benefit, whereby performers were permitted to choose the programme for specific benefit nights when they also kept any profits from ticket sales. The only benefit performance of a Shakespeare play attended by Soane took place on 5 June 1817. On this evening, *Macbeth* was given at Covent Garden for the benefit of Charles Kemble who played Macduff. This was a highly significant occasion on two levels: in theatrical terms it saw the final performance on stage together of J. P. Kemble and Sarah Siddons as Macbeth and Lady Macbeth, two of their most acclaimed Shakespearean roles (Fig.3). On a personal level, it marked for Soane, as he recorded in his notebook, the first occasion he had attended a play since his wife's death in November 1815. Soane had, however, made a rare visit to the opera on 19 February 1817 when a performance of *The Marriage of Figaro* was given at the King's Theatre.

The Shakespearean text which the audience heard was very different from that used in modern productions. From the late 17th century, the plays were subject to adaptation and rewriting to produce acting versions which held the stage well into the nineteenth century despite scholarly editions being printed. There was, however, awareness, at least amongst critics, of significant and undesirable changes to language, plot and character. In a review of *The Tempest* revived on 8 December 1806 and seen by Mrs Soane on 19 December, the critic of the *Morning Post* expressed strong disapproval. 'We cannot but regret that the

Left: Fig. 3 Soane's ticket to J.P. Kemble's retirement dinner on 27 June 1817, SM Private Correspondence I.K.4.3

Manager...has preferred the Tempest as altered by Dryden, to the original written by Shakespeare. The introduction of an additional daughter of Prospero's, and the Prince [Hippolito?], totally destroys the simplicity ... and diminishes greatly the interest of ... Miranda and Ferdinand.' He goes on to state that the 'indecent' dialogue introduced by Dryden and Davenant which might have been popular in the reign of Charles II '...the present decorum of society renders inadmissible.'[2] Equally subject to drastic amendment was *King Lear* attended by Soane in 1794. A version adapted by Nahum Tate in 1681 virtually held the stage until 1838 and included amongst other changes, Lear regaining his throne, the omission of the Fool and Cordelia avoiding death and marrying Edgar. The *Katharine and Petruchio* seen by Mrs Soane in 1806 was a version of *The Taming of the Shrew* much reduced by David Garrick in 1754 and performed into the 1840s.

Music usually held a significant place in Shakespearean production as was emphasised in a review of *Macbeth* with Kean in the title role first presented in November 1814 and attended by Soane in May of the following year. The music, then attributed to Purcell was said by the reviewer to have '...contributed its full share to the general success of the play. It was so well received that the witches, at the end of the second act, could hardly escape an encore...delightful airs and choruses ... were sung to perfection.....A new Overture by Mr John Horn, introduced the Play, and Scotch Airs, extremely well adapted were played between the acts.' A rare comment on the appearance of the scenery is also included in the same review which stated that: 'In beauty and in fitness it could not be surpassed. The gallery in Macbeth Castle and the exterior of the Castle itself are particularly entitled to commendation. The rocky pass, with a bridge over which Macbeth passes when he first enters, was very much admired...'[3]

From depictions of the performers in Shakespeare plays in Soane's time, it appears that a gradual, albeit uneven move towards semi-historical costume and away from contemporary dress took place. In relation to *Macbeth*, a double portrait of 1786 by Thomas Beach of J.P. Kemble and Sarah Siddons as Macbeth and Lady Macbeth, the actors appear to be dressed in contemporary, fashionable silks and velvets and furs. In contrast, about twenty years later, a satirical print of 1809, *A parody on Macbeth's soliloquy at Covent Garden Theatre* depicts Kemble in a kilt and sporran with a length of tartan cloth across his shoulder. This presumably represents the style of costume Kemble wore at his final appearance as Macbeth which Soane witnessed in 1817. As part of the movement towards historically-based costume, it seems to have been acceptable to employ both contemporary and historical costume simultaneously. The production of *Katharine and Petruchio* (*The Taming of the Shrew*) which Mrs Soane saw at Covent Garden in 1806 is reflected in a print of 1802 which depicts the hero in a 'historical' slashed doublet and breeches with a large feathered hat, whilst the heroine wears a contemporary high-waisted dress.

Neither John nor Elizabeth Soane recorded any comments on the actors and actresses they saw in Shakespearean roles. From the many who achieved great success at the time, the reputations of only a handful, such as Sarah Siddons, J. P. Kemble and Edmund Kean survive today (Fig.4). Fortunately, performances were often the subject of detailed reviews which discussed the actors' presentation of character through the interpretation of text, vocal qualities, gesture and facial expression. Such reviews and descriptions in newspapers, magazines and memoirs provide an impression of the stage performances experienced by the Soanes. In *King Lear*, the first Shakespearean production attended by Soane on 12 May 1794 it was said of Alexander Pope in the title role, '...none have excelled, except Mr. Pope...' and '...in supporting the feebleness of age, he did not forget that tremulousness of voice, so essentially necessary to give reality to the scene, however difficult to the Actor'.[4] Pope's performance as Othello was seen by Soane on 17 September 1794 and described the next day as '...a masterpiece of Tragic acting: his sonorous and powerful voice gave admirable effect to the declamatory parts of the jealous Moor'.[5]

In choosing to see *Hamlet* on 4 September 1807 Soane witnessed an actor, Charles Mayne Young at the beginning of a highly successful London career. The reviewer of the *Morning Post*, 23 June 1807 was impressed with Young's approach to this iconic character. '...the exultation which he displayed the success of his scheme to discover the guilt of Claudius; the tenderness with which he moralized on the skull of Yorick; the burst of passion in which he addressed Laertes, at the grave of Ophelia... During the evening the audience repeatedly and rapturously testified their sense of his merit...'

An actor whom Soane saw five times in Shakespearean roles was Edmund Kean whose compelling interpretation of Richard III was witnessed by Soane on 5 December 1814. Kean's first performance in the role was described by a reviewer in *The Times* of 4 October 1814 who described the performance towards the end of the play. 'The gradual recovery of reason, the proud resumption of faculties that had so reluctantly given way to terror, and the lofty contempt with which a daring spirit might spurn itself for yielding to the influence of a dream, wound up this display and shed addition lustre round the actor who could sustain and embody and illusion so trying and so noble.'

In contrast to such lavish praise, reviewers could be brutally honest even with the greatest of performers. Soane saw Sarah Siddons as Lady Macbeth, probably her most admired Shakespearean role, on 5 June 1817. Having formally retired in 1812 she occasionally returned to the stage and in a detailed critique of this performance the reviewer states: 'Her voice is somewhat broken since last year; her articulation of some words... is defective and her delivery of the principal passages is unequal, slow, improgressive and sometime inaudible. Her pauses too were long and frequent...In a word she appeared to act rather from memory than from present impulse; and to be deficient in that lofty decision and force of manner, which used to characterise her.' Present at the same performance was the young actor William Macready (see Fig.1) who, though agreeing that Siddons presented 'a mere repetition of the poet's text' evokes something of the power and creativity which Kemble, after a slow start, eventually brought to the performance, his last as Macbeth. In the final act, Kemble 'with the inspiration of despair' gave the Tomorrow and tomorrow speech 'rising to a climax of

Right: Fig. 4 Francis Bourgeois, *Mr Kemble as Coriolanus, Act IV, Scene I*, 1797, SM P99

desperation that brought down the enthusiastic cheers of the closely-packed theatre ...At the tidings of "the wood of Birman moving," he staggered as if the shock had struck the very seat of life...His shrinking from Macduff when the charm on which his life hung was broken ...was a masterly stroke of art...'[6]

On 19 August 1820 the entry in Soane's notebook (Fig.5) reveals that he indulged in an unusually splendid evening culminating in a Shakespearean performance of the highest quality. Before the theatre, Soane, together with a friend, the sculptor Charles Rossi, consumed a dinner costing about 15s 6d (£1 was worth £86) in Paternoster Row at Dolly's Chop House which was noted for its beefsteaks. Soane also paid 14s, the price of two box seats at Drury Lane so that they could see *Othello* in some comfort. The performance of Kean in the title role had been the subject of overwhelming praise in an earlier review. 'Kean as Othello, was perfection itself. Unreservedly throwing himself into the part, he gave full scope to his genius ...In the third act he transcended himself; and on the whole a more sublime display of nature was never presented by the histrionic art.'[7]

Soane's notebooks record no more visits to the theatre. Kean's magnificent performance was therefore not only the final play Soane attended but a fitting culmination to his experience of Shakespeare in the theatre.

Emmeline Leary is an independent scholar.

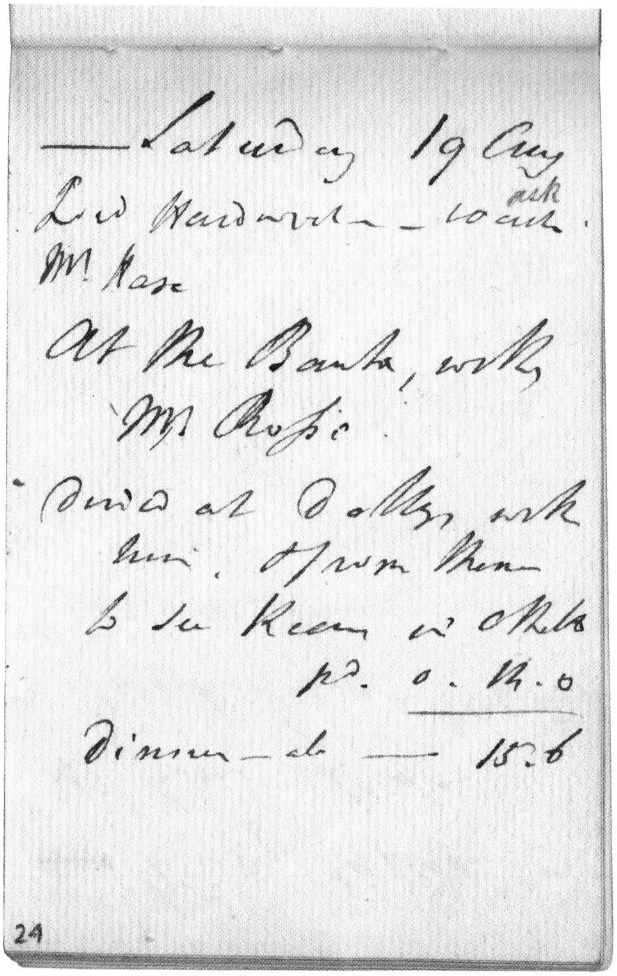

Fig. 5 The entry in Soane's notebook for 19 August 1820. SM SNB 159

Endnotes

1   The *Morning Post*, 9 December 1806.
2   The *Morning Post*, 13 December 1806.
3   The *Morning Post*, 7 November 1814.
4   The *Morning Post*, 7 January 1794.
5   The *Morning Post*, 18 September 1794.
6   ed. Sir Frederick Pollock, *Macready's Reminiscences*, New York, 1875.
7   The *Morning Post*, 8 July 1820.

Performances of Shakespeare plays known to have been attended by John Soane and Elizabeth Soane in London and Liverpool 1794–1820.

Who	Source	Date of Perf	Play	Venue	Extra information
JS	SNB	12 May 1794	*King Lear* with *British Fortitude* and *Netley Abbey*	CG	Expenses of the play 0. 3. 6
JS	AJ	17 Sept 1794	*Othello* with *Netley Abbey*	CG	At the Play 0. 3. 6
ES	ENB	17 Oct 1805	*Macbeth* with *Bon Ton*	DL	
ES	ENB	30 Oct 1806	*Katherine and Petruchio* [*The Taming of the Shrew*] with *Love in a Village*	CG	To see Love in a Village
ES	ENB	19 Dec 1806	*The Tempest* with *Arbitration*	CG	With Mrs L cost 6s
JS	AJ	4 Sept 1807	*Hamlet* with *The Dramatist* and *Music Mad*	H	Hamlet by Young [Charles Young 1777-1856]
JS	AJ	19 Oct 1807	*Romeo and Juliet* with *The Forty Thieves*	DL	At the play with Mrs S 0. 7. 0
JS/ ES	SNB ENB	9 Aug 1810	*Othello*	L'pool	[G. F. Cooke played Iago]
JS	SNB	5 Dec 1814	*King Richard the Third* with *The Ninth Statue*	DL	Went to see Kean in Richard, the first time
JS	SNB	3 May 1815	*Macbeth* with *The Ninth Statue*	DL	At the play with Miss P[atterson?]
JS	SNB	3 July 1815	*King Richard the Third* with *Past Ten o'clock and a Rainy Night*	DL	At the play, Kean , Richard 0. 8. 6
JS	SNB AJ	5 June 1817	*Macbeth* with *Raising the Wind*	CG	AJ Went to see Macbeth Mr [J.P.] Kemble and Mrs Siddons, Charles Kemble's Benefit 1. 10 .0 (1st time of going to a play)
JS	SNB	6 July 1820	*The Merchant of Venice* with *Giovanni in London*	DL	I went to see Kean in Shylock
JS	SNB	19 August 1820	*Othello* with *Modern Antiques*	DL	Dined at Dolly's with Mr Rossi and from there to see Kean in Othello pd 0. 14. 0 , dinner ab. 15. 6

Play		JS	ES
1	*Hamlet*	1	
2	*King Lear*	1	
3	*King Richard III*	2	
4	*Macbeth*	2	1
5	*Merchant of Venice*	1	
6	*Othello*	3	1
7	*Romeo and Juliet*	1	1
8	*Taming of the Shrew* (as *Katharine and Petruchio*)		1
9	*Tempest*		1

Notes

Who: JS = John Soane,   ES = Elizabeth Soane

Source: SNB= J Soane Notebooks   AJ= J Soane Account Journal   ENB= Elizabeth Soane Notebooks

Venue: CG= Theatre Royal, Covent Garden   DL= Theatre Royal, Drury Lane H= Theatre Royal, Haymarket as identified in contemporary newspapers.

Extra information = information included in Sources e.g. prices of tickets; the pit was 3s 6d